U.S. ARMED FORCES

The U.S. MARINE CORPS

MICHAEL BENSON

LERNER PUBLICATIONS COMPANY / MINNEAPOLIS

CHAPTER OPENER PHOTO CAPTIONS

Cover: A marine in full dress uniform stands at attention during a military academy parade.

Ch. 1: Marines arrive for training at Fort Ternate, the Philippines, in amphibious assault vehicles.

Ch. 2: U.S. Marine recruits pledge to defend the United States.

Ch. 3: During boot camp, marine recruits perform grueling physical exercises, including hundreds of sit-ups, push-ups, and pull-ups at a time.

Ch. 4: U.S. and Filipino marines participate in a joint training exercise. Joint exercises are crucial in developing international cooperation and a unified fighting force.

To John Freeze

Acknowledgments
Thanks to Tim Treu, David Jacobs, Jake Elwell, Sergeant David Curry, and Peg Goldstein

Lerner Publications Company
A division of Lerner Publishing Group
241 First Avenue North
Minneapolis, MN 55401

Website address: www.lernerbooks.com

Library of Congress Cataloging-in-Publication Data

Benson, Michael.
    The U.S. Marine Corps / by Michael Benson.
        p.   cm. — (U.S. Armed Forces)
    Includes bibliographical references and index.
    ISBN: 0-8225-1648-9 (lib. bdg. : alk. paper)
        1. United States. Marines—Juvenile literature. I. Title: United States Marines. II. Title.
    III. Series: U.S. Armed Forces (Series : Lerner Publications)
    VE23.B45 2005
    359.9'6'0973—dc22   2004002962

Manufactured in the United States of America
1 2 3 4 5 6 – JR – 10 09 08 07 06 05

Contents

chapter ONE

HISTORY

NICKNAMED "FIRST TO FIGHT" because they are often the first U.S. military force on the scene of battle, U.S. Marines are some of the toughest fighters in the world. Marines fight on water, on land, and in the air. They specialize in amphibious assaults—arriving by sea and then fighting on land.

The U.S. Marine Corps is the largest group of marines in the world, with more than 170,000 members on active duty. The corps is divided into two forces: one based along the Atlantic Ocean at Norfolk,

Virginia, and the other based in the Pacific Ocean at Pearl Harbor, Hawaii.

In addition to fighting in wars, U.S. Marines protect U.S. naval ships and other military sites along the U.S. coast. They guard U.S. embassies (diplomatic offices) around the world. The U.S. Marine Corps is part of the Department of the Navy, and the U.S. Marines and U.S. Navy often work together. For example, navy ships transport marines to their missions in other parts of the world. Many marine and naval officers train together.

EARLY AMERICAN MARINES

The history of the U.S. Marine Corps dates to the American Revolution (1775–1783). During this conflict, North American settlers fought to free themselves from British rule. In 1775 American leaders created a marine corps, called the Continental Marines. The corps

A full regiment of Continental Marines rushes into battle. Their drums bear the famous slogan Don't Tread on Me.

was modeled after the Royal Marines of Great Britain, formed in 1664.

Stationed aboard naval ships, the Continental Marines became the Revolution's "soldiers of the sea." The ships were equipped with large, powerful guns called cannons. Sometimes marines boarded British ships. There, they fought enemy marines and sailors at close range using rifles, pistols, swords, and bayonets—sharp blades attached to the ends of their rifles.

In their first battle, the Continental Marines captured New Providence Island, an island in the Caribbean Sea, from the British. The marines also fought alongside the Continental Army—the American ground forces—at other important Revolutionary battles. During the war, the Americans created a new nation, the United States of America. It established a small marine force, the U.S. Marine Corps, in 1798. Major William Burrows became the corps commander.

THEY'RE CALLED LEATHERNECKS

During a conflict against the French at the end of the 1700s, U.S. marines began wearing black leather collars *(above)* as part of their uniform. The collars protected the marines' necks during sword fights. Although the collars were dropped from the marine uniform in 1872, marines are still known as "leathernecks."

In the early 1800s, the marines saw action in North Africa. Pirates based in Tripoli, in modern-day Libya, were attacking U.S. ships on the Mediterranean Sea. U.S. Marines arrived in Tripoli in 1805. They marched across the desert to defeat Tripoli's rulers. The "Marines' Hymn," written in the mid-1800s, refers to marines fighting on "the shores of Tripoli."

Marines again fought against the British in the War of 1812 (1812–1815). During this war, marines fought naval battles on the Great Lakes and the Atlantic Ocean. Marines also helped army general Andrew Jackson defeat the British at the Battle of New Orleans, the last battle of the war.

The marines headed south to fight in the Mexican War (1846 to 1848). They landed on the eastern and

Marines fought fierce battles on the Mediterranean Sea during the war with Tripoli.

western coasts of Mexico and came ashore to help the U.S. Army defeat the Mexican army. "From the halls of Montezuma," another line from the "Marines' Hymn," refers to the victory in Mexico.

The Civil War (1861–1865) split the United States into two halves: North and South. Marines fought for the North, called the Union. Along with the army and navy, marines attacked Southern forces, coming ashore from ships along the Atlantic coast. They also fought battles on the Mississippi River and at Bull Run in Virginia. The South, known as the Confederacy, formed its own marine corps during this war. In 1865 the South surrendered to the North, reuniting the nation and ending the Civil War.

Marines took part in the Spanish-American War of

DANIEL DALY

One of the most famous marines of the early 1900s was Daniel Daly *(above)*, who won two Medals of Honor. Daly earned his first medal in 1900 in China, during a conflict called the Boxer Rebellion. He earned his second medal 15 years later in Haiti, when he and 34 other marines fought off more than 300 Haitian rebels.

During World War I (1914–1918), Daly fought heroically in France. As first sergeant of the 73rd Machine Gun Company, he led a famous charge at the Battle of Belleau Wood. He earned the Navy Cross and the French Victory Medal for his heroism.

After World War I, marine general John Lejeune said, "Daly is the outstanding marine of all time." General Smedley Butler, the only other marine to win two Medals of Honor, called Daly "the fightin'est marine I ever knew."

1898, helping Cuba gain its independence from Spain. In keeping with their "first to fight" reputation, the marines were the first U.S. force to land in Cuba during the conflict. During the first part of the 1900s, marines also fought in the Philippines, China, Nicaragua, Mexico, Haiti, and the Dominican Republic.

WORLD WARS

World War I took place in Europe between 1914 and 1918. During this war, Germany and its allies fought against Great Britain, France, and many other European nations. Siding with the French and British, the United States entered the fighting in 1917.

U.S. Marines fought many land battles during the war. They fought in France at the battles of Belleau Wood, Soissons, Saint-Mihiel, and others. Some marine pilots fought midair battles called dogfights. Using machine guns, they tried to shoot down enemy airplanes from the sky. The war ended with Germany's defeat.

Fresh troops silently march to their position in France during World War I.

WOMEN IN THE MARINES

Women first joined the Marine Corps as office workers *(above)* in 1918, during World War I. The Marine Corps needed female office workers because men were needed for battle. The female marines were called Marinettes. When the war ended, women were not allowed to remain in the Marine Corps.

Women served in the Marine Corps again during World War II (1939–1945). Nicknamed Lady Marines, these women worked as photographers, airplane mechanics, welders, painters, telephone operators, and in other noncombat jobs. When World War II ended, the women were again sent home. But not for long. In 1948 the Marine Corps allowed women to join the force along with men.

At first, female marines were not allowed to hold combat jobs. Gradually, the marines opened more and more combat positions to women. In the 2000s, female marines can serve as combat pilots and in other dangerous jobs. Only three jobs are still off-limits to women: serving as foot soldiers, firing big guns called artillery, and invading beaches in amphibious assault vehicles.

World War II (1939–1945) began when Germany invaded many of its neighbors in Europe. In 1941 Germany's ally Japan attacked Pearl Harbor, Hawaii, and the United States entered the war. Marine divisions went to the Pacific Ocean to fight the Japanese. The marines used amphibious invasions to attack islands held by Japanese troops.

U.S. companies built special equipment and weapons to help the marines and other U.S. soldiers. Small boats called landing craft could carry marines from big ships to the beach. Planes called dive-bombers swooped down and dropped bombs on the enemy.

Before each attack, navy ships fired shells onto beaches where the marines were going to land. They tried to destroy any enemy troops or weapons on the beach. Then marines came ashore in landing craft. Once they controlled the beaches, the marines fought the Japanese farther inland. Marines

Marines raise the U.S. flag on Mount Suribachi in Iwo Jima during World War II. This famous photograph was the basis for a monument to the Marine Corps in Arlington National Cemetery near Washington, D.C.

used rifles, machine guns, cannons, grenades, and flamethrowers.

The Marine Corps' roughest fight of World War II (and its roughest battle ever) was the Battle of Iwo Jima. Iwo Jima is a tiny island in the Pacific Ocean. In 1945 the island was held by Japanese soldiers, who hid in tunnels under the ground. The United States wanted to capture the island and use its airfields. From there they could launch bombing attacks on nearby Japan.

The U.S. attack on Iwo Jima took place in February and March 1945. More than 70,000 marines landed on the island. More than 6,000 of them were killed in the attack, and about 13,000 were wounded.

The marines suffered many casualties—soldiers killed and wounded (above)—in the fight to capture the island of Iwo Jima during World War II.

The first black man known to fight with the marines was John Martin, also called Keto. A slave in Wilmington, Delaware, he fought in the American Revolution. But African Americans were not officially allowed to join the marines until World War II. Even then, they had to serve in all-black units, commanded by white officers. In 1948 the United States ended racial segregation (separation of white and black troops) in the military. By the Vietnam War in the 1960s and 1970s, black and white marines fought side by side. In the 2000s, one out of every five marines is African American *(above)*.

But the Americans captured the island, killing most of the 22,000 Japanese defenders.

The final—and largest—battle in the Pacific took place on Okinawa, a southern island of Japan. Tens of thousands of marines invaded the island. They fought on the ground and dropped bombs from the air. Almost 3,000 marines were killed in the battle. Close to 12,000 more were wounded. But the United States captured the island. Soon after the battle, the United States dropped atomic bombs on the Japanese cities of Hiroshima and Nagasaki, killing thousands of people. The Japanese surrendered in September 1945. The fighting in Europe had ended a few months before. World War II was over.

MORE FIGHTING IN ASIA

The United States fought in Asia again during the
Korean War (1950–1953), when North Korea invaded
its neighbor South Korea. The United States came to
the aid of the South Koreans. Marine ground and air
units played a major part in the war. They invaded
enemy shores and fought inland, just as they had done
in World War II. But during the Korean War, they
traveled from ship to shore in helicopters as well as
landing craft. Helicopters were much faster than
landing craft and could drop off and pick up marines
far inland, even behind enemy lines. The war ended in
a stalemate. North and South Korea agreed to exist
side by side as a divided nation.

In the 1960s, the United States tried to help South
Vietnam in a civil war with North Vietnam. The

Marines move swiftly among rice paddies (fields)
during the Vietnam War.

conflict was called the Vietnam War (1954–1975). Marines and other U.S. soldiers had a difficult fight in Vietnam. Enemy troops hid in jungles, set exploding booby traps, and made surprise ambushes. The enemy was determined, and tens of thousands of U.S. soldiers were killed. During the early 1970s, U.S. troops slowly pulled out of Vietnam. After the Americans left, the North Vietnamese won the war.

A marine breaks down in tears while dodging sniper fire after the 1983 suicide bombing of a U.S. Marine base in Beirut, Lebanon.

THE WAR ON TERROR

During the 1980s, terrorists from the Middle East repeatedly struck out against Americans. One of the worst attacks occurred in 1983, and U.S. Marines were the victims. The marines had been sent to Beirut, a city in Lebanon, to help keep the peace during a civil war. On October 23, a suicide bomber drove a truck packed with explosives into a marine base near the Beirut airport. The resulting blast killed 241 marines.

Marines saw more action in the Middle East when Iraq, led by dictator Saddam Hussein, invaded its

More than 90,000 marines fought in Operation Desert Storm
(1991), more than in any other conflict before or since.

neighbor Kuwait in 1990. The marines were part of an
international force that came to Kuwait's rescue in
1991. In this conflict, called Operation Desert Storm,
the soldiers used new kinds of weapons, such as laser-
and satellite-guided bombs. These weapons could hit
their targets with pinpoint accuracy. The Americans
and their allies easily defeated the Iraqis, taking very
few casualties.

Terrorists flew passenger planes into buildings in
New York City and Washington, D.C., on September 11,
2001, killing about 3,000 men, women, and children.
The marines were quick to respond. The attacks were
traced to a terrorist group called al-Qaeda, based in
Afghanistan. The corrupt government there protected
the terrorists. Marines and other U.S. forces went to

Afghanistan and quickly defeated its government. But the war against al-Qaeda continues and some marines are still fighting in Afghanistan.

In the winter of 2003, the United States once again went to war in Iraq. This time U.S. forces went to topple Saddam Hussein's government. Marines and other U.S. forces used new high-tech weapons, such as "smart bombs," to hit targets precisely without damaging nearby buildings. The major fighting ended after a few weeks. Many marines remain to help Iraqis rebuild their nation.

In early 2004, marines were sent to the Caribbean nation of Haiti. The country was in chaos. Armed rebels had taken to the streets. The president, Jean-Bertrand Aristide, had resigned. The marines came to restore peace and order. Soon, troops from other nations arrived to help the marines keep the peace.

Marines destroy weapons found in an Iraqi truck. Destroying enemy weapons is part of the ongoing campaign in Iraq.

chapter TWO

RECRUITMENT

THE U.S. MARINE CORPS wants
members who are well educated and in top physical
condition. The marines also want members who have
pride in themselves and pride in their country. Finally,
the marines want members who are willing to fight.
History shows that marines are more likely to see
combat than servicemen and servicewomen in other
branches of the U.S. military.

Not everyone is cut out to serve with the marines. In
fact, in advertisements, the corps promotes itself as "the

few, the proud, the marines." Standards for enrollment are very high. People who want to join the marines must be in top physical condition and must achieve high scores on a military intelligence test. Even those who make it to basic training don't necessarily become marines. Many drop out because the training is so tough.

This marines poster advertises how tough it is to be a marine.

ENLISTING IN THE MARINES

A person who wants to enlist in (sign up for) the Marine Corps must be a high school graduate. He or she must be a U.S. citizen or a resident alien (a citizen of a foreign country living legally in the United States). The person must also be in good physical and mental health and must be between 17 and 28 years old. But 17-year-olds need their parents' permission to join.

Enlisting in the marines is a big commitment. Many young people visit with a high school guidance counselor to discuss the decision to join. Everyone who wants to enlist must meet with a recruiter at a local Marine Corps recruiting office. Recruiting offices are found in most big U.S. cities. At the meeting, the recruiter will give the candidate detailed information about the Marine Corps. The recruiter will help the candidate decide whether to join. Newly enlisted marines are called recruits.

All recruits must take a test called the Armed Services Vocational Aptitude Battery (ASVAB). This multiple-choice exam tests recruits' language, math, mechanical, and other skills. Those who do poorly on the test will not be admitted into the Marine Corps.

Some recruiters visit schools and community centers, sharing information about the Marine Corps and looking for future recruits.

For those who pass, the test helps the Marine Corps determine what military job the recruit will be best suited for. The marines try to match recruits with jobs they want—and with jobs the corps needs to fill. Recruits who do very well on the ASVAB are eligible for the most elite jobs in the Marine Corps, such as military intelligence, satellite communications, and aircraft maintenance positions.

THE MARINE EMBLEM

To show that marines can fight on land, on sea, and in the air, the official Marine Corps emblem *(above)* combines a globe, an eagle, and an anchor.

OBLIGATIONS AND BENEFITS

After acceptance into the Marine Corps, newly enlisted marines must sign a contract with the U.S. government. With this contract, recruits agree to serve in the marines for four years. After four years are up, marines can reenlist for two, three, or four more years.

In return for serving their country, the Marine Corps gives recruits a paycheck, housing, food, health care, and other services. The Marine Corps also helps marines go to college. For instance, after serving in the marines, a student can receive money for paying college fees. Other programs help marines pay off old college loans or earn college credit while they serve in the marines.

Some people choose to spend their entire careers with the marines. These marines reenlist time and again. Their pay increases over time. After 20 years, marines can retire with a full pension. This means the government gives them a monthly payment, health insurance, and other benefits until they die.

THE MARINE RESERVES

Some people choose to join the Marine Corps Reserve, a force of part-time marines. Many reservists also have full-time jobs, while others are full-time students. Usually, reservists serve one weekend per month and two weeks every summer. But reservists must agree to become full-time marines in case of emergency, such as during wartime. During the 2003 war in Iraq, many marine reservists were called into active duty.

The requirements for joining the Marine

Marine reservists can be called into action at any time.

22

Marine Corps officers form battle plans and give orders to other marines.

Corps as a reservist are the same as those for joining as an active-duty marine. And the training is every bit as tough.

MARINE CORP OFFICERS

The leaders in the Marine Corps and other military branches are called officers. Officers plan military strategy and tell other marines what to do in combat and noncombat situations. Most marines who become officers do so by enrolling in special officer-training programs.

Unlike the other branches of the U.S. military, the Marine Corps does not have its own military academy, or officer-training college. But some Marine Corps officers receive their training by attending the U.S. Naval Academy in Annapolis, Maryland, the U.S.

Military Academy in West Point, New York, or the U.S. Air Force Academy at Colorado Springs, Colorado. All are four-year colleges.

These military academies are three of the best colleges in the world. It is very difficult to get into these schools. To apply, candidates need a letter of recommendation from a member of Congress or another high-level government official. Candidates must be between 17 and 23 years of age, U.S. citizens, and unmarried. They must also have graduated near the top of their high school class.

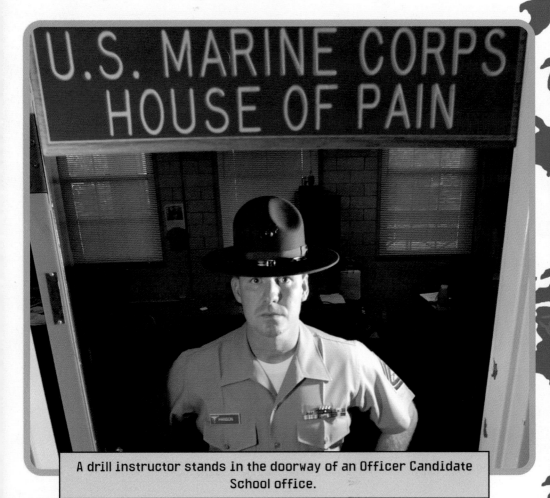

A drill instructor stands in the doorway of an Officer Candidate School office.

Students at military academies learn about military history, mathematics, engineering, foreign languages, and communications skills. They also learn about cultures from around the world and about current issues, such as terrorism. Students also undergo an intense physical fitness program.

After graduation from a military academy, marine officers receive more training at the marine officer-training program at Quantico, Virginia. Here, both

A female marine crawls through a trench as part of her physical training program at Quantico, Virginia.

outdoors and in the classroom, officer candidates are taught to think under pressure. They learn about military history and strategy, how to command others, and how to work for a commanding officer. They also learn advanced war-fighting skills— everything an officer needs to know to lead a marine force into battle. Graduates enter the marines as second lieutenants.

UNIFORMS

ON-DUTY MARINES must always be in uniform. You can tell a marine's name, rank, and job by a quick glance at his or her uniform. Marines have several different uniforms for different occasions, jobs, and situations. These outfits include dress uniforms and combat uniforms.

COMBAT UTILITY UNIFORM

Marines wear combat utility uniforms when they're in combat, on patrol, or in other battle situations. This uniform has a camouflage design, which helps a marine blend in with his or her background, whether it be the forest, the jungle, or the desert. The trousers are loose fitting and tuck into the tops of a marine's boots. Jackets have a lot of pockets for quick access to gear. The combat helmet is made of a bulletproof material called Kevlar and is covered with camouflaged canvas.

SERVICE UNIFORMS

On leave, on indoor duty, or any time
marines are away from the battlefield,
they wear plain green service uniforms.
This uniform includes a flat-top green hat
with a visor, a tan shirt and tie, green
trousers, and a belt. The uniform varies
according to the weather. In hot weather,
it includes a short-sleeved shirt. In cold
weather, it includes an overcoat.

"DRESS BLUES"

For formal occasions, such as
ceremonies, marines wear their "dress
blues," a blue suit with a wide belt worn
outside the coat. This uniform comes
with a flat-brimmed hat, cuffed trousers,
black dress shoes, and white gloves.
Female marines have the option of
wearing trousers or skirts.

"THE MARINES' HYMN"

From the halls of Montezuma,
     to the shores of Tripoli,
We fight our country's battles in the air,
     on land and sea.
First to fight for right and freedom,
     and to keep our honor clean:
We are proud to claim the title
     of United States Marine.

Our flag's unfurled to every breeze
     from dawn to setting sun.
We have fought in every clime and place,
     where we could take a gun.
In the snow of far off northern lands
     and in sunny tropic scenes,
You will find us always on the job,
     the United States Marines.

Here's health to you and to our Corps
     which we are proud to serve.
In many a strife we've fought for life
     and never lost our nerve.
If the Army and the Navy ever look
     on heaven's scenes,
They will find the streets are guarded by
     the United States Marines.

Most Marine Corps officers do not attend a military academy, however. Instead, most receive their training through the Naval Reserve Officer Training Corps (ROTC) program. More than 60 colleges and universities in the United States offer this program, which trains both navy and marine officers. To qualify, a student must achieve a high score on an intelligence test, pass a thorough physical examination, and be admitted to a school that has the Naval ROTC program.

Two ROTC cadets (students) take a break while running an obstacle course. Like enlisted marines, cadets have to pass tough physical fitness examinations.

In addition to regular college classes, students in the ROTC program learn about warfare, military history, and leadership skills. Marine officer candidates attend a special "marine option" of the program. Between freshman (first) and sophomore (second) year, students take a six-week summer training course aboard a navy ship or at a naval base. Between junior (third) and senior (fourth) year, students attend the Officer Candidate School in Quantico, Virginia. Students who graduate from the marine program of Naval ROTC enter the marines as second lieutenants.

chapter THREE

TRAINING

AFTER ENLISTING and taking the
ASVAB, Marine Corps recruits report for basic
training, also called boot camp. Male recruits who live
east of the Mississippi River take basic training at
Parris Island, South Carolina. Male recruits who live
west of the Mississippi train in San Diego, California.
All female recruits train at Parris Island. Male and
female recruits train separately at boot camp, but their
training is mostly the same.

The first week of boot camp, marines go through

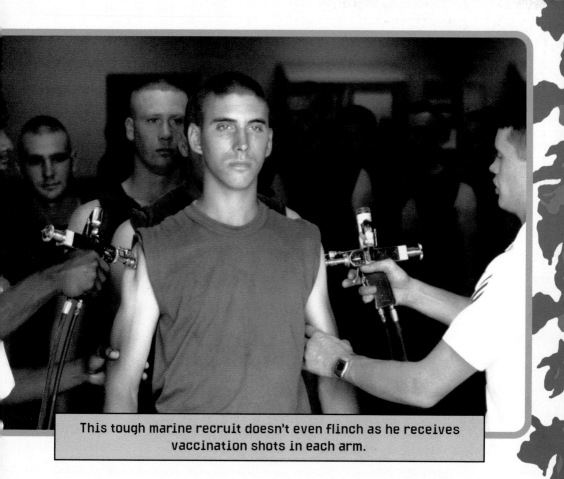

This tough marine recruit doesn't even flinch as he receives vaccination shots in each arm.

processing. They fill out a lot of forms, get a full physical exam, and receive shots from a Marine Corps doctor. The Marine Corps wants all recruits to dress and look alike, so that they think of themselves as part of a team, not as individuals. So at processing, male recruits get a marine haircut, which is just shy of complete baldness. Female recruits do not have their heads shaved. They must wear their hair short or pinned up neatly. Recruits also receive uniforms and toiletry items, such as soap and shampoo. They keep these things in small sacks called ditty bags.

TRAINING RECRUITS

Marine boot camp is tough, both physically and mentally. Only three out of four recruits who enter boot camp finish the program. Many cannot handle the grueling training and drop out. Others fail their tests.

Drill instructors (DIs) are in charge of teaching recruits during boot camp. DIs are tough but not cruel. Their job is to make recruits strong, physically and mentally. Male DIs train male recruits. Female DIs train female recruits. All DIs wear the same wide-brimmed "Smokey Bear" hats. The DI's job is to turn recruits into marines—to make them some of the toughest, strongest fighters in the world. The recruit's job is to obey all the DI's commands right away. No questions asked.

DIs are very tough on recruits. They make sure that recruits are mentally and physically strong enough to be marines.

Boot camp lasts 13 weeks. During this time, recruits learn all the basic skills they'll need to be marines. They learn to operate weapons, march across rough terrain, and swim in the ocean. Some of the most important skills they learn are how to get along with people who are different from them and how to work as part of a team.

Recruits also learn to do everything they are told, quickly and willingly. They learn to treat all marines and fellow recruits with courtesy and respect. They learn to be completely fair and honest in everything they do. They learn to respect the rights and property

Marine recruits perform jumping jacks as part of their training. Plenty of exercise ensures the marines stay in top shape.

of others, to be proud of themselves and their uniforms, and to work hard to strengthen their bodies. Most important, recruits learn *never* to quit.

During boot camp, recruits wake up at 5:30 in the morning and go to bed at 9:00 at night. Much of the first few weeks in book camp is dedicated to physical training: running (with boots on) and long sessions of exercise. When recruits are not working out, they march and drill. The

Climbing up a long rope is one of the many tough activities recruits must master during boot camp.

Marine Corps wants recruits to act as a team. So recruits learn to turn in step with other marines. They learn how to throw their rifles from shoulder to shoulder with precision, at exactly the same time as everyone else in line. Recruits also study in the classroom. They learn about military history and Marine Corps traditions. They learn the rules of international warfare, such as the proper way to treat prisoners of war.

Marines spend a lot of time training with their M16A2 rifles. This rifle is equipped with a bayonet (knife) attachment.

About halfway through boot camp, recruits begin rifle training. A recruit will rarely go anywhere without his or her M16A2 rifle. Recruits spend a lot of time every day making sure their rifles are in top condition. This means regularly cleaning their rifles. Recruits also take them apart and put them back together again to make sure all the parts are in good working order. Recruits learn to fire their rifles accurately, hitting targets at distances up to 500 yards away. At the end of rifle training, recruits take a shooting test. Most marines pass the test on their first try. Those who don't pass must practice and try again.

After rifle training comes a week of field, or battle, training. During this week, recruits learn what it's like to go to war and how to operate on a battlefield.

Wearing a 50-pound backpack most of the time, recruits learn to fire a pistol, throw hand grenades, walk through minefields, and handle other battle situations. Field training is followed by "crucible week," a tough week of simulated (mock) combat.

Hand-to-hand combat exercises teach marines how to survive in battle situations.

TOOLS OF THE TRADE

MARINES USE A VARIETY OF WEAPONS and machines in their work. These weapons are constantly being improved to be state of the art.

GUNS

Marine infantrymen (marines who carry rifles and fight on the front lines) use the light and accurate M16A2 rifle, which can be fitted with a bayonet. They also use grenade launchers, devices that attach beneath the barrel of a rifle. A grenade launcher can shoot a grenade at a target up to 225 yards away—a lot farther than a marine could throw a hand grenade. Marines also use machine guns. Machine guns can fire more than ten bullets per second and hit targets up to two and a half miles away.

JETS

The F/A-18 fighter jet *(below)* can fly almost twice the speed of sound (about 1,400 miles per hour). This jet can shoot missiles and drop bombs. The Harrier jet, or "jump jet," can take off and land like a helicopter, straight up and down. Once in the air, it can shoot and drop bombs like a fighter jet. It can fly 690 miles per hour (a little less than the speed of sound).

HELICOPTERS

Sea Cobra *(right)* attack helicopters are armed with cannons and missiles. Sea Knight and Sea Stallion helicopters transport marines from ships into battle. All three kinds of helicopters can take off from the deck of an aircraft carrier, a ship with a runway for aircraft.

COMMUNICATIONS SYSTEMS

Based on trucks, ground mobile communications systems *(left)* can send messages from the battlefield to anyplace else in the world. The messages travel via satellites, which are spacecraft that circle Earth. Satellites, lasers, and computers are also used to guide bombs and missiles to their targets. These "smart weapons" are able to hit targets with pinpoint accuracy.

Marines stand at attention during their boot camp graduation ceremony in Parris Island, South Carolina.

At the end of boot camp, recruits are tested in all the skills they have learned to that point. Testing takes place both in the classroom and outdoors. Those who pass their tests receive a brand-new uniform and officially become U.S. Marines.

ADVANCED TRAINING

After two weeks off, marines on the East Coast go to Camp Lejeune, North Carolina. Marines on the West Coast go to Camp Pendleton, California. There, marines receive four more weeks of battle training. Some training takes place in the classroom, and some takes place outside. Recruits learn battlefield tactics, camouflage techniques (learning to blend in with the background to be a difficult target), map reading, and survival skills.

Next, each recruit takes specialized training for one of 350 Marine Corps jobs. Some marines go to pilot school. Others go to driving school. Mechanics head for a garage. Communications specialists learn to operate message-sending equipment. Depending on what specialty he or she chooses, a recruit's job training will take from three weeks (for a file clerk) to eighty weeks (for someone learning to repair missiles and missile guidance systems). Most training programs take about eight weeks. Advanced training takes place at different military bases around the country, depending on the job.

Marine mechanics keep all equipment running smoothly, from tanks to amphibious assault vehicles to helicopters. This mechanic checks the hydraulic system of an AH-1W Cobra helicopter.

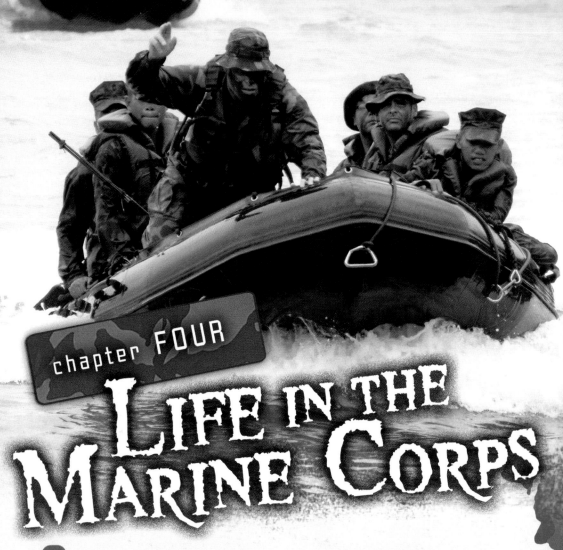

LIFE IN THE MARINE CORPS

AFTER TRAINING IS OVER, marines report to a base, where they will do the work they have trained for. The base assignment will depend on the marine's job and the needs of the Marine Corps.

Marine bases are like small cities, complete with stores, hospitals, schools for marines' children, courthouses, churches, and jails. The Marine Corps has about 20 major bases in the United States. It also has bases in Japan and Europe and new bases close to the fight against terrorism in Afghanistan and Iraq. Some

The Marine Corps has bases in all parts of the world.
This marine base is in Okinawa, Japan.

marines are based aboard naval ships. Most marines
live on base and sleep in barracks, big dormitories with
bunk beds. Some veteran marines (those who have been
in the corps a long time) live near their bases in houses
or apartments. Marines with families often live with
them in family-housing facilities.

A marine's day-to-day life will depend a lot on the
job he or she has chosen and trained for. Some marines
operate radios and other communications tools. Some
code and decode messages. Some marines construct
buildings and roads. Others work at computer repair,
aircraft maintenance, or law enforcement.

INSIGNIA

LIKE ALL OF THE U.S. ARMED FORCES, the Marine Corps is organized according to rank. A person of lower rank is required to follow the orders of someone of higher rank. For example, a private, the lowest rank, is expected to follow the orders of a master sergeant or captain. A captain is required to follow the orders of a major or colonel and so on. The highest Marine Corps rank is four-star general.

All members of the Marine Corps wear insignia, or symbols, that show their rank. Here are some marine insignia, starting with the lowest rank and moving up to the highest.

ENLISTED PERSONNEL

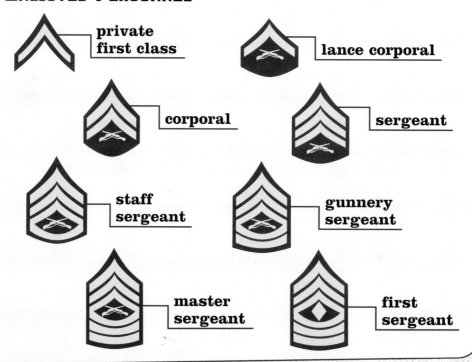

private first class

lance corporal

corporal

sergeant

staff sergeant

gunnery sergeant

master sergeant

first sergeant

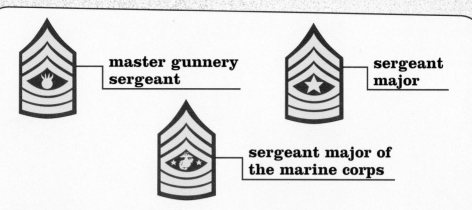

master gunnery
sergeant

sergeant
major

sergeant major of
the marine corps

OFFICERS

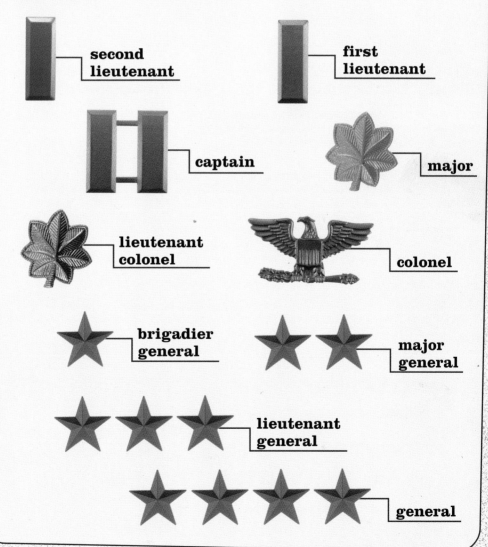

second
lieutenant

first
lieutenant

captain

major

lieutenant
colonel

colonel

brigadier
general

major
general

lieutenant
general

general

Infantrymen prepare to fire an M224 60mm Lightweight Company Mortar System (LWCMS).

JOBS IN THE INFANTRY

Infantrymen are marines who carry rifles and fight on the front lines. They are the backbone of the Marine Corps. Only men can become infantrymen, since only men are allowed to fight on the front lines.

Each member of the infantry has a specialty. Some fire machine guns.

Infantrymen are the backbone of the Marine Corps. Only men can become infantrymen, since only men are allowed to fight on the front lines.

Others are experts at firing antitank missiles. A gifted sharpshooter—able to hit distant targets with accuracy—might work as a sniper. A gifted swimmer might work as a diver, attaching underwater explosives and tracking devices to enemy boats. Some marines work in reconnaissance. They sneak behind enemy lines and gather information about the enemy. Others are airborne troops, who specialize in parachuting into battle.

LIFE ON BASE

A marine's typical day, especially on base, might go something like this: A marine corps mapmaker, stationed at a base in the United States, might get up at 6:00 A.M. This is when the camp bugler plays a tune called "Reveille." She will shower, dress in her service (work) uniform, and eat a quick breakfast before reporting for duty at 7:30.

Her work might involve making maps of Iraq, where

A camp bugler proudly plays "Reveille."

marines will be traveling with gasoline and other supplies. She'll create new maps using a computer, existing maps of Iraq, photographs taken by U.S. spy planes and satellites, and written reports.

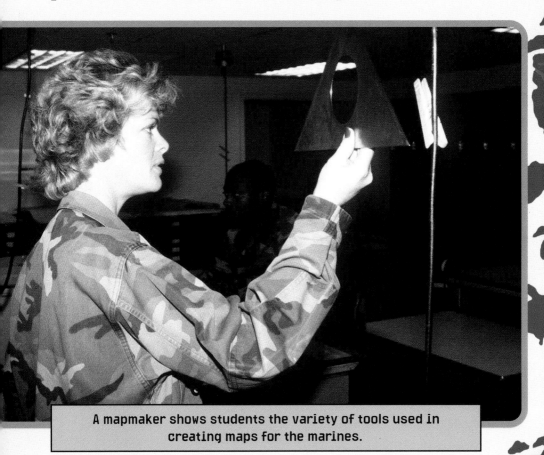

A mapmaker shows students the variety of tools used in creating maps for the marines.

After a break for lunch in the base mess hall (dining room), the marine might meet with her mapmaking unit, then continue creating maps at her computer. After dinner at 5:00 P.M., her time is her own. Of course, the daily routine will vary for each marine, depending on his or her job and base, and whether it is wartime or peacetime.

LIFE IN COMBAT

A marine's life in combat is very different from life on base. There is nothing routine about being at war. Each day is different from the one before. During a battle, a marine usually doesn't sleep or eat in the same place twice.

During the 2003 war in Iraq, marines had some of the toughest jobs. They were in charge of capturing the Iraqi village of Nasiriyah, where fighting was very heavy. In Baghdad, the Iraqi capital, marines went from block to block, looking for pro-Hussein fighters

An injured marine is transported aboard a stretcher after receiving injuries during the fighting in Nasiriyah, Iraq, in 2003.

U.S. Marines break down a door in Baghdad as part of their campaign to capture important areas of the city in the 2003 war in Iraq.

holed up in empty buildings. About 18 miles north of Baghdad, marines discovered and took control of a large bombproof underground complex. It turned out to be an Iraqi nuclear facility, with high levels of radiation, a harmful form of energy. When the major fighting ended, marines took on the dangerous job of policing Baghdad. Later, U.S. Army soldiers replaced the marines in this work.

THE FUTURE OF THE MARINES

What will the U.S. Marine Corps be like in the future? We can't know for sure. But some things about the

Marine Corps will never change. The pride of the Marine Corps will never change. And the way marines are used in U.S. military actions will remain the same. The Marine Corps will still be amphibious. That is, marines will usually come from the sea and attack on land.

The future Marine Corps will have faster and larger helicopters so more marines can move from ships into battle in just minutes. Those same choppers will take wounded marines from the battlefield to the hospital in record time.

U.S. Marines will continue to use new technology, such as satellite communication systems. Using satellite- and laser-guided weapons systems, marines will be able to attack enemy troops. They will almost never miss the target—and without hitting civilians. New amphibious assault vehicles will carry marines across both water and land.

Sea Knight helicopters often carry marines to and from their missions.

MARINE ONE

When the U.S. president travels across the country or to another part of the world, he usually flies in a special jet called Air Force One. But sometimes the president needs to travel shorter distances very quickly. At these times, he rides in a marine helicopter known as Marine One. This chopper can pick up the president on the White House lawn and get him to Andrews Air Force Base in Maryland within minutes. The marines also provide helicopters for the vice president and for visiting world leaders, if necessary.

Marine One has room for a crew of four (a pilot, a copilot, a crew chief, and a communications officer) and 10 passengers. Marine One is designed for both business and comfort. Inside, it looks like a comfortable office. A ride in Marine One is like riding in an "air limousine."

Marine One has two engines and can fly in any type of weather. If Marine One is needed across the country or in a foreign country, it doesn't have to fly there itself. Its two rotary blades fold up. Then it can be quickly loaded onto a cargo plane.

In the future, the Marine Corps will supply more and more of its own air support during attacks. Marine jets will shoot at the enemy from the air before the start of a ground attack. Less help from the air force or navy will be needed.

Some things will remain the same. The training to become a marine will always be tough. During boot camp, every marine will still get a taste of just how tough the job is going to be. Every marine will always be in top physical condition, a warrior ready for battle. And we can always count on the Marine Corps to be filled with tough and proud Americans.

In early 2004, marines were called to Port-au-Prince, Haiti, to control unrest there.

STRUCTURE

THE BASIC MARINE UNIT IS THE SQUAD, made up of 12 marines. Four squads make up a platoon, four platoons make up a company, and four companies make up a battalion. Four to six battalions make up a regiment. Three regiments make up a division, and two or more divisions make a corps.

Each of these units is led by an officer, starting with a sergeant for a squad and moving onto a lieutenant for a platoon, a captain for a company, a lieutenant colonel for a battalion, a colonel for a regiment, a major general for a division, and a general for a corps.

Generals report to the Marine Corps commandant, a four-star general and the highest-ranking marine. The corps commandant reports to the secretary of the navy, who reports to the secretary of defense, who reports to the president of the United States.

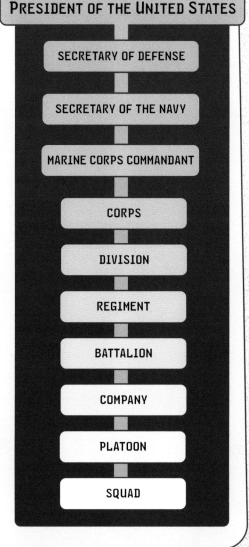

PRESIDENT OF THE UNITED STATES

SECRETARY OF DEFENSE

SECRETARY OF THE NAVY

MARINE CORPS COMMANDANT

CORPS

DIVISION

REGIMENT

BATTALION

COMPANY

PLATOON

SQUAD

TIMELINE

1775	The Continental Congress, an early U.S. lawmaking body, creates the Continental Marines.
1776	The Continental Marines win their first battle when they raid and take control of New Providence, an island in the Bahamas.
1801–1805	Marines fight and defeat forces in Tripoli in North Africa.
1812–1815	During the War of 1812, marines fight the Royal Army and Navy of Great Britain.
1846–1848	During the Mexican War, marines fight a series of battles with Mexico.
1861–1865	During the Civil War, the U.S. Marine Corps fights on the side of the Union (North). The Confederacy (South) creates its own marine units.
1898	During the Spanish-American War, marines battle against Spanish soldiers for control of Cuba and the Philippines.
1917–1918	In World War I, marines fight a series of battles in France against German troops.
1941–1945	In World War II, marines fight Japanese troops on islands in the Pacific Ocean.
1950–1953	During the Korean War, marines assist South Korea in its fight against North Korea.
1960s	In the Vietnam War, marines fight alongside South Vietnam against North Vietnam.
1983	More than 200 marines die in Beirut, Lebanon, when a terrorist blows up a marine barracks.
1991	In the Persian Gulf War, marines help drive Iraqi troops out of Kuwait.
2001	Marines go to Afghanistan to fight al-Qaeda terrorists.
2003	Marines invade Iraq and help overthrow Saddam Hussein.
2004	Marines help keep the peace during unrest in Haiti.

GLOSSARY

ammunition: material, such as bullets and shells, fired from guns and artillery pieces

amphibious: operating on both land and water

camouflage: patterned clothing or other material that allows soldiers to blend in with a natural background

casualties: soldiers lost during warfare due to death, injury, sickness, or capture

civilian: a person not involved in military service

combat: active fighting in warfare

infantry: soldiers trained and equipped to fight on foot

insignia: a badge or symbol, often showing military rank

reconnaissance: exploring enemy territory to gain information

satellite: a spacecraft that orbits Earth, often equipped with communications equipment, cameras, and other devices

terrorism: the use of violence, such as bombing, to frighten and kill civilians instead of soldiers

FAMOUS PEOPLE

F. Lee Bailey (born 1933) Bailey was born in Waltham, Massachusetts. During the 1950s, he served in the marines as a pilot. He later graduated from Harvard University and Boston University Law School. He went on to become a famous defense lawyer, working for O. J. Simpson and other suspected murderers. He has also written books, including *The Defense Never Rests*.

Patty Berg (born 1918) Born in Minneapolis, Minnesota, Berg became a pioneer in the world of women's golf. She began playing golf at age 13. After winning 29 tournaments as an amateur, she turned pro in 1940. During World War II, she served in the marines as a lieutenant. Berg later helped found the Ladies Professional Golf Association (LPGA) and won 57 tournaments on the LPGA tour. In 2003 she was inducted into the Marine Corps Hall of Fame.

Gregory Boyington (1912–1988) Gregory "Pappy" Boyington was an ace Marine Corps aviator during World War II. Born in Saint Maries, Idaho, Boyington enlisted in the Marine Corps in 1935. There, he learned to fly airplanes. In 1941, before the United States entered World War II, Boyington left the marines and joined the Flying Tigers, a group of volunteer aviators who helped China in its fight against Japan. He rejoined the marines in 1942 and took command of the famous Black Sheep Squadron. Fighting in the Pacific, Boyington shot down 22 Japanese aircraft in the fall of 1943. In January 1944, his own plane was shot down, and he spent a year and a half as a Japanese prisoner of war. Boyington was awarded the Congressional Medal of Honor, the nation's highest military honor, for his wartime heroism.

Roberto Clemente (1934–1972) Born in Carolina, Puerto Rico, Clemente joined the Marine Corps in 1958 as an infantryman. He served full-time until 1959 and remained in the reserves until 1964. A baseball Hall of Famer, Clemente won four National League batting titles and was named the league's Most Valuable Player in 1966. He died in a plane crash while flying supplies to earthquake victims in Nicaragua.

Sarah Deal (born 1969) Deal, a graduate of Kent State University in Ohio, was the first woman in the marines to fly combat vehicles. Born in Pemberville, Ohio, Deal graduated from Kent State with a degree in aerospace flight technology. She joined the Marine Corps in 1992 and began studying air traffic control. When the U.S. secretary of defense lifted a ban on women flying combat vehicles in 1993, Deal began pilot training. She earned her wings in 1995. Deal flies the Sea Stallion, the largest helicopter used in the military. She is also active in community DARE (Drug Abuse Resistance Education) programs and was named one of "350 Women Who Changed the World 1976–1996" by *Working Woman* magazine. She was also featured in a Learning Channel documentary titled *Gender Wars* and a Discovery Channel show called *Flightline*.

Ronald Lee Ermey (born 1944) Born in Emporia, Kansas, Ermey served in the U.S. Marine Corps from 1961 to 1972. When injuries forced him to retire from the corps, he moved to the Philippines, where he studied criminology and drama at the University of Manila. While there, he landed his first role in a Hollywood film, *Apocalypse Now*. Ermey has since appeared in more than 50 films. He received a Golden Globe nomination for his role in *Full Metal Jacket* in 1987. Ermey's work also includes voice roles in the *Simpsons*, *Toy Story*, and the video game *Crash Bandicoot: the Wrath of Cortex*. In 2002 he became the host of the History Channel's popular *Mail Call*.

John Glenn (born 1921) Born in Cambridge, Ohio, Glenn became a marine lieutenant in 1943. Trained as a pilot, he flew 59 combat missions in the Pacific during World War II. He also flew combat missions during the Korean War. Glenn later became a test pilot and then an astronaut. In 1962 he became the first American to orbit Earth in a spacecraft. He was elected a senator from Ohio in 1974, serving for 24 years. In 1998 Glenn returned to space aboard the space shuttle *Discovery*. Then aged 77, he was the oldest person ever to travel in space.

Gustav Hasford (1947–1993) Born in Russellville, Alabama, Hasford joined the marines in 1967. He worked as a combat correspondent in Vietnam, writing news reports from the battlefield. He then used his experiences to write *The Short-*

Timers, a novel about the Vietnam War. The novel became the basis for a 1987 film, *Full Metal Jacket,* directed by Stanley Kubrick. Hasford was nominated for an Academy Award for developing the screenplay for the movie. He later wrote two more novels, one about Vietnam, another a detective story.

Lee Marvin (1924–1987) Marvin, a Hollywood actor, was born in New York, New York. Best known for his lead role in *The Dirty Dozen,* a 1967 war movie, Marvin also won an Oscar as Best Supporting Actor in the western comedy *Cat Ballou* in 1965. Marvin enlisted in the marines at the start of World War II and served in the Pacific. He was wounded during the Battle of Saipan in 1944 and received the Purple Heart medal. He is buried in Arlington National Cemetery near Washington, D.C.

Carol A. Mutter (born 1940) Born in Greeley, Colorado, Mutter served in the Marine Corps for 31 years. She was the first woman to command a fleet marine force and the first female marine lieutenant general. She is best known for her work with the U.S. Space Command, an organization that conducts joint space operations with the marines and other military branches. Mutter retired from the Marine Corps in 1991.

John Philip Sousa (1854–1932) Nicknamed the March King, Sousa was a famous American composer and bandleader. Born in Washington, D.C., Sousa studied music as a young man. He played violin with theater and dance orchestras and composed a variety of music, including operettas, songs, and waltzes. In 1880 Sousa became the leader of the U.S. Marine Corps Band, a position he held for 12 years. He wrote several marches for the band including the famous "Semper Fidelis."

BIBLIOGRAPHY

Alexander, Joseph H. *The Battle History of the U.S. Marines: A Fellowship of Valor.* New York: Harper Perennial, 1999.

Hunt, George P. *The Story of the U.S. Marines.* New York: Random House, 1978.

Lawliss, Chuck. *The Marine Book.* New York: Thames and Hudson, 1988.

Metcalf, Clyde H. *A History of the United States Marine Corps.* New York: G. P. Putnam's Sons, 1939.

Moskin, J. Robert. *The U.S. Marine Corps Story.* New York: McGraw-Hill, 1977.

Simmons, Edwin Howard. *The United States Marines: A History.* Annapolis, MD: Naval Institute Press, 1998.

FURTHER READING

Cornish, Geoff. *Battlefield Support.* Minneapolis: Lerner Publications Company, 2003.

Cureton, Charles H. *The U.S. Marine Corps: The Illustrated History of the American Soldier, His Uniform, and His Equipment.* Langhorne, PA: Chelsea House, 1999.

Dartford, Mark. *Bombers.* Minneapolis: Lerner Publications Company, 2003.

———. *Fighter Planes.* Minneapolis: Lerner Publications Company, 2003.

———. *Helicopters.* Minneapolis: Lerner Publications Company, 2003.

———. *Missiles and Rockets.* Minneapolis: Lerner Publications Company, 2003.

Feldman, Ruth Tenzer. *The Korean War.* Minneapolis: Lerner Publications Company, 2004.

Kennedy, Robert C. *Life in the Marines.* Danbury, CT: Children's Press, 2000.

Levy, Debbie. *The Vietnam War.* Minneapolis: Lerner Publications Company, 2004.

Lurch, Bruno. *United States Marine Corps.* Portsmouth, NH: Heinemann Library, 2004.

Marte, G. F. *U.S. Marine Corp Special Forces: Recon Marines.* Mankato, MN: Capstone Press, 2000.

Sherman, Josepha. *The Cold War.* Minneapolis: Lerner Publications Company, 2004.

Williams, Barbara. *World War II: Pacific.* Minneapolis: Lerner Publications Company, 2005.

WEBSITES

Naval Reserve Officers Training Corps
<https://www.nrotc.navy.mil>
Students interested in joining the Marine Corps as officers can train at a college NROTC program. This site includes a list of schools with NROTC programs, as well as information about scholarships and applications.

U.S. Marines
<http://www.usmarines.com>
This site gives detailed information about jobs in the Marine Corps, marine history, and more.

United States Marine Corps
<http://www.usmc.mil>
This site contains information regarding marine recruiting, units, careers, and news, plus biographies of top marine officers.

Women Marines Association (WMA)
<www.womenmarines.org>
The WMA is an association of female Marine Corps veterans. The group's website offers current and historical information about women in the marines.

Index

ABOUT THE AUTHOR

Michael Benson is the former editor of the *Military Technical Journal* and *Warzone* magazine. He is also the author of 30 books, including *The Alpha Bravo Delta Guide to Warplanes* and *Complete Idiot's Guide to Submarines and Aircraft Carriers.* Originally from Rochester, New York, he is a graduate of Hofstra University. He lives with his wife and two children in Brooklyn, New York.

PHOTO ACKNOWLEDGMENTS

The images in this book are used with the permission of:
© U.S. Naval Photos provided by Navy Visual News Service, Washington D.C., pp. 4, 13, 17, 24, 26 (right), 42; © National Archives, pp. 5, 6, 9, 11, 12, 14; © Library of Congress, p. 7; © www.homeofheroes.com, p. 8; © Bettmann/CORBIS, p. 10; © U.S. Marine Corps, pp. 15, 19, 20, 22, 33, 35, 44 (all), 45 (all), 47, 51, 53; © Defense Visual Information Center, pp. 23, 36, 38 (top), 39 (all), 40, 41, 43, 46, 48; © Leif Skoogfors/CORBIS, p. 18; © Sam Lund/Independent Picture Service, pp. 21, 27 (all); © U.S. Department of Defense, pp. 16, 38 (bottom); © Anna Clopet/ CORBIS, pp. 25, 34; © Todd Strand/Independent Picture Service, p. 26 (left); © Bohemian Nomad Picturemakers/CORBIS, p. 29; © Anne Griffiths Belt/CORBIS, p. 31; © Bob Krist/CORBIS, p. 32; © David H. Wells/CORBIS, p. 37; © Michael Macor/San Francisco Chronicle/CORBIS, p. 49; © Christophe Calais/In Visu/CORBIS, p. 50; © Tim Graham/CORBIS, p. 52.

Cover: © Michael S. Yamashita/CORBIS.